Turtle Light Press Haiku Chapbook Contest Winners

The Window That Closes, Graham High (2013)

All That Remains, Catherine J.S. Lee (2011)

Sketches from the San Joaquin, Michael McClintock (2009)

Other Turtle Light Press Haiku Books

Nick Virgilio: A Life in Haiku, Nick Virgilio
(Edited by Raffael de Gruttola)

Peace and War: A Collection of Haiku from Israel, Rick Black

Also by Graham High

POETRY

Ravens of Unresting Thought, Outposts Publications
Attempts to Love, Athenaeum Books, Hub Publications
No Turning Back, Ram Publications
Wolf on the Third Floor, New Hope International Publishers
The Range-Finder's Field Glasses, Oversteps Books

HAIKU

Between the Heartbeats, Ram Publications
Where Two Streams Meet, Ram Publications
Towing the Breeze, Ram Publications
Once Around the Sun, Ram Publications
Under the Edge of the Horizon, Ram Publications
36 Views of King's College Chapel, Ram Publications
(with Tony Eva's photos)
A Bigger Ocean, Ram Publications
Wave on Wave, Ram Publications

HAIBUN/PROSE POETRY

Travelling Light, Ram Publications

TRANSLATIONS

The Enigma, Haiku by Tomas Tranströmer, Ram Publications
(Translated from Swedish to English)

EDITED VOLUMES

Dover Beach and My Backyard, International Haibun Anthology,
British Haiku Society
Barbed Wire Blossoms, Museum of Haiku Literature Award
Winners Anthology, British Haiku Society

෴

The Window That Closes

Graham High

The Window That Closes

Turtle Light Press • Arlington, Va. • 2013

2013 Turtle Light Press Trade Paperback Edition

Copyright © 2013 by Graham High

Published in the United States by Turtle Light Press, LLC

All rights reserved. No part of this book may be used or reproduced without written permission except in the case of brief quotations embodied in critical articles and reviews. To print or reproduce individual poems, please contact Graham High at www.grahamhigh.info; to print or reproduce artwork, please contact Turtle Light Press at info@turtlelightpress.com

ISBN 978-0-9748147-4-2

First Edition

Book cover and interior design by Rick Black
Front cover photo by Rick Black

Turtle Light Press
P.O. Box 50162
Arlington, VA 22205
U.S.A.

www.turtlelightpress.com
info@turtlelightpress.com

In memory of my mother, June High, who first kindled my love of literature and art—and whose own poems and paintings I still treasure.

high hospital bed
my mother and I must cross
the rift of waiting

anxious perspective
my old Mum views the flight path
through the ward window

sun rays filter through
the petrol station flowers
her thin eyelashes

spots of April rain—
the clinic parking machine
rejects my small change

outside for a smoke
I gaze at the yellowed star
we know as Venus

the sun in decline
between two lines of trees
beyond her window

The Window That Closes

all sounds alarm her—
the tea trolley's dull rumble,
distant church bells

back home, she's calmer—
gone the workman's rock-hammer
and the woodpecker

out to see the spring,
she notes the coldness of wind
through thinning hair

through the plane tree,
sun on her old, mottled hands—
bird songs rise and fall

Mum in the May breeze—
the straw in a blue-tit's beak
becomes unwieldy

The Window That Closes

containing the wind
the tumbling, empty, crisp bag
just passes her by

a seat in the park—
now she can hardly manage
that awkward ice cream

empty garden chair
a money-spider inspects
abandoned crochet

a tentative walk—
steadied steps under the leaves,
over the leaves

a special trip
to see the cemetery
his name not so clear

hand on his headstone
the rosettes of dry lichen
and her liver spots

glare of the TV
she asks why war reporters
wear such dark shades

a fresh incident—
her grasp of the newspaper,
the spill of hot tea

through her evening doze,
the kettle steams in the dark—
a grey hair floats down

her hands clasped
in the attitude of prayer
to release a moth

from her back window
a jigsaw of fallen leaves—
some almost fitting

veiled in thin mist,
the walker outside her door
just her son's footsteps

framed in autumn rain
a neighbour meets her gaze from
a facing window

the cat on her lap—
an ear flicks forward every
time she turns a page

her shaking hand—
the dipped biscuit falls slowly
into the tea cup

The Window That Closes

scrawl of winter trees
fills the window by her desk
the diary's blank page

stopped mid-sentence—
remembering something
she can't quite recall

mother and her cat:
two clocks out of sync
but still together

on her windowsill
a line of last week's tea bags—
prospect of dry hills

layers of grey rain
her hours are divided
by memories

just below the moon
the small circle of her breath
in the window frost

"Bluer than the sky!"
she notes the birch tree's shadow
settled on the snow

from her window,
pine needles fallen on snow
yet more snow falling

after her last sigh,
I sketch her face with all
the time in the world

The Window That Closes

a cold empty walk
from her bed to the window
from window to bed

her room bare now—
a moth inside the window
tries to reach the moon

carpet underlay
the nineteen sixties headlines
chewed by silverfish

dusty rectangles
where her paintings used to hang
I close the door slowly

bronze urn patina
a little dust covering
my mother's ashes

About the Author

Graham High first became interested in haiku during 1999. Since then he has had eight collections of haiku published and one collection of haibun. He edited the British Haiku Society Journal, *Blithe Spirit*, from 2005 - 2008 and is currently the Society's President. He came to haiku rather late in his writing career following a life-long commitment to all forms of poetry and creative writing. He has had four collections of poetry published in the UK to date and gives periodic public readings of his work.

In his professional life, he is most active as a visual artist and his creative practice covers both painting and sculpture. As a painter, he has exhibited in a great many group shows and has had more than 40 one-person expositions both in the UK and internationally. In 1989 he was one of the first artists to be invited to hold a personal exhibition in post-Soviet Russia. As a sculptor, he is more traditional and works primarily in bronze. He is active principally in the field of portraiture and wildlife sculpture. In 1994, he was elected an associate member of the Royal Society of British Sculptors and has received many public commissions for his work.

Alongside this activity, he has fitted in a parallel career for 25 years as an Animatronic Model Designer in the Feature Film Industry working on approximately 35 mainstream films including *Aliens*, *The English Patient*, *Babe*, *Labyrinth*, *The Flintstones*, *101 Dalmatians* and the *Harry Potter* series. His contributions to in-front-of-camera special effects have been mainly in the field of animatronic creature effects but have also encompassed prosthetic make-up, miniature sets and character design.

In 2005, he decided that *The Golden Compass* would be his last film in the realisation that computer graphics were replacing the areas previously occupied by physical effects and he has since enjoyed being able to produce a more concentrated output of painting and writing. In his personal life, he is married to Frances and shares his time in the UK between his two homes: one in southeast London, the other on the sea coast of north Norfolk.

For more information about his work, please visit his website:

www.grahamhigh.info

Acknowledgements

I am grateful to the editors of the following publications for the small number of individual haiku that have been published before, some in an earlier version, in *Blithe Spirit, Candelabrum, Haiku Canada, Modern Haiku, Presence* and *Time Haiku*.

I should also like to thank Rick Black for all the time, energy and sensitive suggestions that he has offered and which have contributed to the book in its final form. He is certainly the best of editors.

Lastly, I would like to thank Rick Black and Kwame Dawes for their selection of this manuscript and for judging the haiku competition.

September 2013
London, England

Colophon

As usual, especially with small publishers, sometimes it takes a little longer to publish a book than expected—especially a publisher whose mascot is a turtle.

The body of this book and poems are set in Goudy Old Style; the cover font is Monotype Corsiva. The cover and interior photos on pages 5 and 18 were taken by Rick Black while he was on vacation in Milford, Pennsylvania, where he and his family rented a lovely cottage whose windows reminded him of an English country home that seemed perfect for this book. An interior image of his mother's home window, which appears before the start of the poems, was digitally sketched by Graham High.

The spelling for this edition follows that of Great Britain given the author's residence there. Rick Black and Kwame Dawes served as co-judges for this chapbook competition.

www.ingramcontent.com/pod-product-compliance
Lightning Source LLC
Chambersburg PA
CBHW020024050426
42450CB00005B/634